Wallex Consulting
Whiteleaf Business Centre
11 Little Balmer
Buckingham
MK18 1TF
www.martinwallace.consulting

Do you know who your customers are?

I can show you.

Martin Wallace

From the writer of 8 Simple Steps to Business Development

Introduction

Do you know who your customers are? Of course you do, if you are already set up in business you undoubtedly have a group of customer who visit you or that you do work for, you don't need any help getting to know them, as I'm also sure that if you are in the process of setting up your business you have an idea of what sort of people that you are trying to attract. But then again what about the customers you haven't met yet, how much do you know about them? Do you know where to find them? Do you know what they look like?

That's what this book is aiming to do, to help you identify who these customers are, to help save you time and money, to ensure that you are focussing your sales and marketing in the right area, allowing you the best possible chance to convert leads into customers.

It's no secret that marketing can be a bottomless pit into which money is thrown and unfortunately can very rarely reap results. In my younger days I worked as a driving instructor, with ambitions of owning a large driving school with lots of instructors working for me, one problem kept coming back, I could get enough work to keep me busy, but not to support another instructor certainly not a fleet of them, so I did what everybody else did, I took out an advert in the yellow pages, I combined that with the yell online site and telephone marketing site, all in all costing me around £5000 for one year. From that I received in total one enquiry, from a man looking for a cheap quote, I didn't get the job. My history and I'm sure many other peoples are filled with this kind of wasted spending, why? Because we didn't know how to target our customers, we didn't think about who they were.

So how will this book help you?

By helping you to put together an avatar of your customer, (no I am not talking about a large blue creature from a James Cameron movie), you may have heard the term before and possibly know what one is, but for the purposes of this book I will explain what I mean. An avatar is a representation of a person or group who your business is specifically targeted towards. It may seem like all we are doing is putting labels down of traits of customers, but I would say that during the course of this book using experience and examples I will show you how to go deeper into each heading to allow you to put together the most accurate picture of your potential customer possible.

To be clear, I did not develop the concept of the Avatar, I learned about it from a digital marketing specialist. When the concept was shown to me I was very much put forward as a digital marketing tool, however I disagree with such a limited view, the avatar works for all typed of sales and marketing, some people already use the concept, most without realising that they are, some using it fully but likely even more only partially applying it, leaving a wide scope for improvement in results.

A few years ago before I started using avatars, I had read James Caan's book, 'The Real Deal' (I have to say, actually quite a good book), while I was reading it he mentioned about the manner in which he got his recruitment business up and running, by profiling a sales companies ideal new recruit, once he had it right he pitched that 'fictional' person, as if he were a real candidate, to a sales company, they agreed to having a meeting with this prospect, so James then set upon the task of actually finding someone who met the profile. I was impressed by the manner in which he created a fictional person and was able to get them an interview. Although I wasn't aware of it at the time James Caan basically created an Avatar, he did the sales companies job for them in identifying who they needed, then he was able to target his search specifically, making that fictional character turned real person his first commission. I wonder how often he used that approach.

This is the power of the avatar, if you pull all the elements together correctly, it will allow you to find your customers, target them and sell to them, the sale itself should be easier because you will already know that the person that you are pitching too is ideally suited to your business and will have use for your products or services.

The Avatar will work by putting together ten subject titles and hammering down into the detail of those titles to build up the picture of your potential customer, weeding out the nonsense, the time wasting, attributes less likely to achieve a sale and most of all allowing you to concentrate the cost of marketing to areas that will actually show a return.

So let's get started with putting together your avatar, then you can start finding your customers.

Chapter 1

Location

Location might seem like a no brainer, such an easy concept, you might think I live in London so I want customers in London, I live in Milton Keynes so I want to target customers in Milton Keynes, easy!

Maybe not, at the time of writing this book, there are over 8.6 million people living in London, now if you happen to own a small barber shop on the Edgware Road, then a potential 8.6 Million customers might be a bit much, although we have a further nine subjects to help us reduce this number, we need to look at it a bit harder first. So a start would be to concentrate on just one small local area.

However your business might not be as local as a barber shop, I used to work for a Nationwide transport company, so my target customer base was at the time around 61 million people. Far too big a group to market to, also although we delivered nationwide we only actually had four hubs around the country, meaning that there were areas that we couldn't collect from very regularly as it depended greatly on were our deliveries were. Meaning we would break down our target area to around a thirty mile perimeter of each of our hubs, making it more likely that we could service those new customers well without outrageous cost to ourselves.

Working now as a freelance business consultant I have the ability to work anywhere in the world, giving me a target market initially of around 7 billion people, which seems like a high starting point. Looking at some limitations, booking appointments in 24 different time zones seems like hard work, along with the fact that although my skills are in business theory, sales and marketing which are all transferable, I don't speak the 6500 different languages of the world, which although the task could be overcome with translators, it seems like a market that is far too wide and varied, so I target my business primarily within the UK, however I am open to a wide variety of English speaking countries. However if I was an accountant, then it would probably find myself limited to the country I live in, as although the job itself can be done remotely, the skills need to be transferable and from what I know, the tax laws vary from country to country.

If you run an online business and you send out products via the mail or parcel carriers, think about postage costs, are there any areas that are too expensive to ship to, are there any import or export laws that's need to be obeyed before shipping into a specific region? What are your carriers turnaround times, how do they vary from region to region or country to country?

If your business is a physical entity, also known as bricks and mortar business, such as a shop or eating establishment, you may need to consider your locality, are you on a high street, near a school, in a local centre or in an out of town retail park, all of these elements can effect who will visit you.

What I am saying is simple, identify what area your customers are in, be as specific as possible, really narrow it down, think about where you can work or where customers are likely to travel from, can you make money working there (potential return on investment), are your skills transferable into that market and most if all make sure that you would want to work there or gain work from that location.

Location forms the basis from which all avatars start, you need to make sure you get this bit correct or the rest of it will fail to be as effective as it needs to be.

Chapter 2

Age

What group is your business aimed at? You might think, 'my business is for everyone,' but likely it's not, there may be elements of your business that appeal to everyone, but then you have to narrow it down to what particular group you are targeting at a specific time, remember it is possible to have more than one avatar, the avatar can be recreated to suit a new campaign or approach. For example, if your business is a cafe, you could argue that everyone visits a cafe at some point. So what I would say is identify elements from step one, what is your locality? If you are near a school or a nursery, you could be looking for drop off traffic during the week, on average that could put your target age group around 20-35.

You also may want to consider when you want your business, using the cafe analogy again, you might find that Thursday afternoons are particularly quiet, so what age group of people are generally around at that time of day, depending upon your area that could be retired people. Early mornings could be young professionals needing a quick bite before work, all times of the day can be better suited to different age groups, figure out when and you better know who.

What does your business do? This can very much effect the age group of your customers, if you run a shop filled with the latest fashions, your client base is very much in the 15-25 bracket, whereas if it's a textiles store the age group will start higher.

If you deal business to business you may think that age doesn't matter, a corporations are ageless, aren't they? Decision makers within companies are people and they are the ones you are targeting, to know who or what level of person you are pitching too can make all the difference in how you go about getting noticed. Priorities change with age, knowing where and when to launch your campaign can make all the difference to get noticed and being successful. Younger people check social media more commonly, meaning if your target person within a company is junior management, then it's possible to be noticed throughout the day, older people check social media later in the evening, that could be the safer time to target the more middle to senior management in that way.

To be successful at profiling you have to be aware that there is a great deal of stereotyping involved, there will always be exceptions to the rules, however when we market, we market to the mass not the exceptions, as we look to make our money count for the best reward. Within my business, I find that age plays a big part as mostly I deal with small to medium sized businesses (SME), often owner operated ones. Using what I know about most SME I target an age group of 30-55, as that is my understanding of the age group who generally run those types of businesses. I understand that there are people younger and older than that group who run their own businesses, I myself was 17 when I started my first business, so I am more than aware of the limitations of targeting such a narrow age group, however I am also aware that whilst I was a young entrepreneur I very rarely was willing to accept advice from anyone, it wasn't until my late twenties that I realised that I didn't know everything and that sometimes it's worth taking advice. So aiming a business advice company at a 25 year old who is thriving on the idea of working for himself and being his own boss is not going to be a good use of my resources.

The 55 cut off is for no other reason than I feel I need an upper bracket and from my experience business people in their late fifties into their sixties usually are either quite successful in what they are doing and aren't looking for help or are more resistant to change what they are doing and as such less likely to accept advice. As I said this is a sweeping generalisation, there are always exceptions to the rules and I will happily work with people of all ages, however when I am trying to achieve the best bang for my buck, I aim for the market with the biggest chance of success.

Better understanding of what you need or want for your business, will help you identify what age group to target for potential customers. By getting this stage correct, it will help you with later sections when you need to find out where to target your sales and marketing approach.

Chapter 3

Gender

Similarly to age, gender profiling requires a good deal of generalising, we are forced to make certain assumptions, such as although men nowadays are entitled to take paternity leave and become primary carer rather than their female counterparts, we still work on the expectation that it is woman who will be off work with kids, so when targeting anything to do with babies, toddlers or childcare we tend to still focus on woman.

But it isn't all generalising, some of it is common sense, if you have a women's clothes shop, then it doesn't make sense spending money promoting it too men unless you are running a specific promotion such as Valentine's Day. The focus of this step isn't however to speak about the type of adverts, but more have you concentrating on what type of person would most benefit or be interested in your product or service. Taking into account factors such as we explored with age, who is likely to fit into your need. Going back to the cafe analogy from earlier, if you are struggling with staying busy on a Tuesday morning, you could be looking to target parent and toddler groups, offering incentives for them to meet at your establishment, thinking about the generalisation made about primary carers, it makes sense to target women with that offer.

Beware of applying too many stereotypes within this step, it is not my intention to offend anyone, there is also no implication of sexism, this step relies on you utilising the best common sense available to you, there is no need to dwell too long on the subject, you may decide the gender has no bearing on the sales and marketing of your product or service, which is also completely fine, it is still a matter that requires consideration.

Within my business I have no preference with who I market to, gender has no relevance within business support these days, however twenty years ago that story might have been different although equally if I was in another industry such as specialist retail then it may have significant bearing.

Chapter 4

Finance

Whether you are selling paperclips or BMW's, advertising or accounting, finance should always be a factor within your avatar. It doesn't matter if you offer finance or payment terms or expect cash up front, your customer has to be able to afford your product or service. I dealt with a client who was eager to open up his own shop, preferably on a busy high street, however his financial forecast didn't look strong, meaning we would have to do everything we could to keep the cost of his property as low as possible. I found a company who negotiates with landlords to rent out their vacant properties for free for a fixed term in order to help the owners avoid empty unit rates from the local authority and allow new businesses to get a good start without massive overheads. This seemed like a perfect solution, the company had just negotiated to take on a large retail unit in my clients prime position, the result of this would have meant that the client would only have had to pay business rates to the council for the length of the tenancy. This should have been a win for me, unfortunately upon investigation it turned out that even the cost of business rates at around £60k per annum would make the situation untenable. Eventually we were able to help the client locate a small retail unit, in a less desirable area which was more affordable. So although the customer knew what he wanted and the company was able to provide it, the customer could not necessarily afford it, which is why you have to consider you ideal customers financial position before you waste time showing them something they can't afford.

It's not just a one way thing either, if you can afford more and you want more, you are less likely to accept less. If you owned a car Hyundai dealership and thought it would be a good idea to advertise in Forbes, you would literally be wasting your money, despite both BMW and Hyundai having their own merits, the person who wants a BMW doesn't want to settle for a Hyundai and the Hyundai customers aren't likely to be reading Forbes.

If you are dealing business to business, then consider what it is you are selling and what industries can really afford your product or actually is it likely that they could have something bigger and better already. Unfortunately not all industries were created equal, to some a piece of software costing £20k is almost no money and may I fact have the customer doubting whether or not it will be fit for purpose and to others it would be an unachievable amount of money and a waste of time to even consider.

When I was working within the transport industry we had been asked by a potential customer to implement a track and trace system, we were very much an analogue company in a digital age at that time, so I sought about getting quotes for said system, one company I spoke to insisted upon sending someone out to see me, never mentioning price once or my expectation of cost, so I agreed to take a meeting. Three people from that company showed up that day for a one hour appointment in which they were determined to sell, unfortunately the quote put forward was for £50k plus the cost of the equipment, which would be £1000 per handset, this was an amount I was not prepared to pay. I knew my company did not have the ability to fund such an expensive system, so the three sales people were sent on their way. Secondly I received a quote via telephone from somebody else who could provide me a system with 95% of the criteria of the previous company but this time the cost was to be £4k with £100 for the more simplistic handsets to do the job.

The moral of that story was that, the first company wasted three peoples time to visit me, offering a product that I really couldn't reasonably afford and despite all the merits of the great system I was miles away from them on affordability. The second offering was to be quicker, more affordable and simpler to use, despite the fact it contained one less function than its counterpart, it was worth saving £46k in set up costs. The second option was also dealt with via phone and email, meaning that the person selling didn't spend time and money traveling to me, so didn't have to recoup that cost within his quote. Assessment of customer affordability is essential to stop you wasting time and money, if the first company had asked me what I envisaged for a budget and I answered with a conservative £5-10k then they would have known that I wasn't a viable customer for their products, had I answered at around £30-40k, then it may have been worth them coming out if they could come down or they felt like they could bring me up.

If you have the ability to offer credit facilities for large purchases that is good, but companies have to be able to afford the repayments, they also have to be stable enough, brand new companies with little or no record of credit or trading will be a bad bet for any company.

The ability to pay for our products and services is the fundamental backbone of selling anything, so take the time to research what type of finances people who buy from you should have available.

By the time you feed this in to your avatar you will now have a picture of your customers, where they live, what age they are, what gender they are and how much money they have, this in itself is a good start and would probably serve you well if you nothing else. However the next tools will help you to really narrow the search and get you to whom you need.

Chapter 5

Decision Maker

Getting your foot in the door with a customer can be hard work, then once you have achieved that goal you can relax a little and get to the pitch, that's the bit you are good at, you know your subject better than anyone, so you pull out all the tricks, show all the best elements of what you are selling, you carry out your big finish, finally you look at the customer with expectant eyes, when they drop the bombshell, 'I just have to check with my boss/wife/husband/mum/dog/priest/etc.' All of your best work carried out and it turns you weren't dealing with the decision maker, meaning you are now relying on this customer to portray your case to the person who will ultimately make the decision, that's where it all falls down, they won't do it as well as you, use your flip chart or PowerPoint, they won't quote you word for word, it'll be the general gist and that will be all, fundamentally you have wasted your time, you sat down with the wrong person. Ok sometimes those people might come back to you to buy, but very rarely, in the case of double glazing salespeople, they ensure all adult parties will be home when they come to pitch, as they know how hard it is to get in the door, so when they do, they want to make the most of it, this is what you need to do.

Failure to ascertain decision making ability gives potential customers the easiest excuse out of committing to a sale, I know this too well, as I was also guilty of utilising it. For fun on a weekend when I was around twenty I would trot round to one or two of the many car dealerships in town to try out the latest model of the best car that they had to offer, I would always make myself look serious and dressed the part, sales executives desperate to make a sale would happily allow me take the car for a test drive, all I knew I would have to do for the privilege would be to endure a 10 to 15 minute pitch at the end of the drive. Inevitably after sitting listening to all the options available in the car and the finance possibilities, they would then move in for the close, 'so what do you think?' It is at that point I would use my tried and tested response;

'Seems good, I just have to chat with my other half about it.'

Bam, sales persons face drops and they know the sale is gone, best part of an hour wasted with someone who isn't in a position to say yes. On one occasion I can remember a sales man trying to bully me into the decision, by insulting my position as a man to not be able to make my own decisions, needless to say even if I had been in a position to buy, it wouldn't have been from him.

So decision makers are important, when dealing business to business it can be tough to ensure decision maker attendance as often there is a longer pipeline for approval than one simple meeting. That being the case it is vital to ascertain what the approval process is so that you are prepared, however this is part of planning your avatar, identifying who the decision maker would be and how you get them to cut out as many steps as possible.

You may be thinking, I run a cafe, no such decision maker issues there, if people are hungry they eat. That may be true, however where do they eat, how much do they eat, how often will they come back, ultimately how much will they spend? If you have a child friendly play cafe then the decision maker in that relationship likely isn't the full time working dad, it may be the frazzled overly stressed mum or it could be the enthusiastic child who likes to play rather than sit and eat. This can change your approach to how you market, if the child is comfortable and not bugging mummy constantly then she is likely to stay longer, spend more, this is putting the power to the child not the mother, so offering options which make the child happy can be your best ploy. Alternatively if you decide the mother has the all the power in the relationship then you might try to market to her other sensibilities, such as children eat free, or free coffee with every sandwich, something that makes her feel that she has a reason to stay longer, spend more or come back.

There is a decision maker in every sale, a good sales person ascertains who that person is quickly and knows where to concentrate their pitch, a great sales person ensures they have the decision maker present in the first place. I have fallen foul of sales tactics in the past, be it limited time offers, people who speak so quickly that you don't realise you are agreeing to something right up until the end and just people who are very charming, as a result of this I have vowed never to make the decision in the room, I ensure sufficient time has passed so I know if it is a good decision to make. But that's not really true, as I buy from shops/online/cafés all the time, I very rarely walk away and come back, occasionally I pick an item up so that there is no chance of someone else buying it whilst I decide, but the chances are if it is in my hand I will likely buy it. My wife is a completely different kettle of fish as she could carry the item all around the store for half an hour and then still put it back rather than buy it. What I am saying however is that there is always a decision to be made and that involves a decision maker, whether they buy in the room or call you two days later with a decision, you need to make sure that all parties needed to say yes are there to hear the pitch otherwise the likelihood of a sale is quite remote.

Identify who the decision makers are within your current customer base, look at the trend and use that information to decide who the decision maker is within your avatar. If you don't have a customer base yet and you are just starting out, think about yourself, your friends and family assess how each of you would make the decision to buy your product.

Chapter 6

Knowledge

If you are in the business of selling DIY particle accelerator kits, you may find that there is a very specific market of people who will buy this product that will mainly be based on their understanding of how to use it and what it is for. Not all products will be understood by everyone, or even if people know what it is, they might not know how to use it or why they would need it. So it becomes your job to ascertain who knows enough about your product to actually buy it.

This element applies to services just the same, I have occasionally found that there are business owners out there that don't understand the function or role of a business consultant, they find themselves confused or worried about an issue within their business, feeling like they are completely on their own, but don't pick up the phone or send an email to someone who can actually help. In most cases people like myself will often do a free initial consultation, in order so that we can determine whether or not we are able to help with the specific issue or sometimes just so we can demonstrate our worth, like a try before you buy.

What is the level of education or knowledge required to buy your product or service, remember you may think its simple but as you are the one involved with selling it, I would expect you to have a good understanding.

Sometimes it can be good to ask friends and family to explain what it is that you do or sell, sometimes you can find that the answers are quite surprising.

I used to work within a digital marketing firm as a business development manager, it was the worst job of my life, mainly because the company itself wasn't entirely sure what exactly it did, or if they knew they couldn't verbalise it into a way that was understandable to other people. We provided applications, software and occasionally the hardware to assist with digital marketing, unfortunately it wasn't until we spoke about specific products or somebody looked at our website that people actually started to understand what it was that we did, which made getting past gatekeepers using telemarketing exceptionally hard, email marketing only worked when getting the email worded correctly and getting it too somebody who understood what it meant.

I accept that for some industries there shouldn't be massive amounts of knowledge required, such as buying a hot drink from a cafe, however, if you are having a special on mocha choco lattes, then you have to be sure that people know what that drink is, the same can be true of retail, my dad has never been technologically minded, he didn't grow up with computers and he has never had a use for them in his adult life, so he is unlikely to be a target customer for the new iPad or tablet, because although he might find the product useful if he was to have one, he doesn't recognise the need or understand how to use it.

They say knowledge is power, but ensuring your target customers already possess the right knowledge can be truly powerful. When profiling your avatar you have to be careful not to just make assumptions such as, everyone knows what a catapult is, or everyone knows Pythagoras theorem or even everyone knows who the Prime Minister is. Nothing is absolute, there will be people with a shocking lack of knowledge, the will be groups of people, even entire towns that may not know certain things, because culturally they may not have had any reason to learn or retain that information. I will say it one more time, just because you know it, don't assume everyone does.

Chapter 7

Technology

Within technology we assess the elements of what/where/when? What do I mean? I hear you ask, I mean simply what technology does your potential customer have access to, where are they when they use it and when do they use it?

This is to do with how you are getting your message out to the customer, are you using the web, SMS, fax, email, social media, carrier pigeon? What medium does your avatar most commonly use, how are you going to get the message out to them about who you are, what you are doing?

Starting with what, after deciphering information about your avatar from earlier sections you are able to make certain assumptions, if it is a young professional you seek then we can assume iPad/tablet, smart phones are an obvious medium. Older professionals might use a laptop or desktop computer still they will probably have access to the more sophisticated of communication devices. Older, lower tech style companies may still be using a fax commonly, opening that up as a possible direct link to their offices. Most businesses and or people have email addresses these days, in the majority of cases these will be checked regularly every day. The majority of people have social media accounts of one form or another, so you will need to figure out which one best suits your avatar (we will come back to social media in more detail later). For the person always on the move, SMS marketing can be very effective, sometimes harder to initiate without some kind of earlier buy in, but that might be how you keep up to date with your avatar. There are so many outlets available to you to get your message out there, try figuring out what will work best for your potential customers.

I have always been a fan of email marketing, it is cheap, not necessarily time consuming and you have the ability to hit a large market very quickly, using services such as mail chimp it is possible to just upload your list, copy and paste your message and hit send, mail chimp will track all the relevant information such as successfully delivered mail and whether or not it was opened. In the past I have used this to great effect, doing a mass mail out may not have gotten me lots of responses, but the ones it did made the process more than worthwhile, however it only really worked with the right kind of company. If you constantly just send out mass emails to everybody, it's like using a machine gun to hit a fly, whereas if you target lesser quantities of companies, more specific to your own requirements, then it like using a fly swatter.

Where does your avatar use the different technology, are they at home, at work, in the gym or in the car? It's fine to assume that these different people have all this different technology, but where are they using it, understanding this will help you decide upon the type of marketing approach that you take, if they are at work then you need a something eye catching, but then you can include more detail if required, if they are at home, it needs to eye catching, but also quickly interesting, buyers need to be brought around quickly, short and to the point is best.

So we know what our avatar has, where they tend to use it, but what about when, although this may seem a little pointless, I can assure you that understanding how your customers engage with technology will allow you to maximise the impact of any digital form of marketing that you carry out. If you come to the conclusion that your avatar uses their tablet at night for social media purposes, then you can target that social media type with adverts that come out in the evening. If your avatar is checking emails midday on a Wednesday, because their style of business is quiet at that time, then that's when your email campaign needs to go out. We all live busy lives, if we receive a sales or marketing message at a time when we are busy or in the wrong place to deal with it, we will likely delete without reading. However if that same message comes out at a time when we aren't busy and are just killing time online, then the results can be very different.

Time, place and style are everything when putting together a marketing campaign, so take some time to figure out what your avatar likes to use, where they are and when they are using it.

Chapter 8

Interests

We now know who our avatar is, where they live, what age and gender they are, how much money they have to spend, we are comfortable that they are the decision maker, we know that they have the knowledge to understand what we do and we know what technology that they have access to. So we know a lot about them, but where can we find them, what do they like, how do we get our message to them?

We do that by looking at their interests, I also realise we are speaking about a fictional person and we can never know everything about them or what all of an individual's interests are, however we can look at what interests they should have to have an interest within our product or service. Why? Because this is how we narrow down our search further, it's how we know where to look for our customers. If you have ever used Facebook ads, you will notice that it gives you options to refine the people who will see your advert, In essence they are asking for your avatar, they want to help you apply some of these elements to make the best use of your advertising money. One of the criteria it asks for are interests, Facebook uses all the information that it has gathered about its members to allow it to focus your campaign solely on those people who would be interested in your product, but you have to set those parameters.

How do we do it? It's very simple really, we use common sense, in the majority of cases, the interests or hobbies that fit in with your product or service are quite obvious, such as when I worked for the digital marketing software company, I set my avatars interests quite wide and simplistic, computers and technology, as I knew that whatever company or individual from a company that we wanted to deal with would have to have an understanding of what we were doing to make it an achievable sale. This feeds off of the knowledge part of the avatar, what do they need to know or experience should they have, so as a result what interests could they have that would give them that knowledge.

When I was doing some work with an online auction company I used a common sense approach yet again making it slightly more specific this time, the avatar would have to have an interest in eBay, Amazon, discount sites, bargains, vouchers and online shopping. The approach allows for a much more targeted campaign meaning that only already potentially interested parties should see the adverts, this approach works especially well when utilising google ads, Facebook, re-marketing and offline marketing approaches.

Look into your own business, what interests are in line with your product or service, if you own a gym then fitness, well-being, nutrition and sport are all good interests to target. Some industries or jobs you may feel don't apply to this method, but I would say if you look hard enough you will find a correlation between interests and customers, I have been working recently with people who have bought into direct selling companies and are trying to grow customer bases and territories, one customer was trying to sell children's books, she couldn't see how a customer's interests would affect her ability to sell. After exploration she could see that although the target market for this product was reasonably large, as were the potential outlets, by focusing in on stay at home parents and organising parties and social gatherings, she was combing an interest in children with a desire for these people to spend time socialising with others, providing a great opportunity to sell books to all the parents.

Paying attention to your customer's interests and combining that with the rest of your avatars traits will narrow down the scope of any advertising, marketing or sales operations, making your endeavours more profitable.

Chapter 9

Pain

Firstly, when I say pain, I'm not endorsing you causing your potential customers harm or threatening them at all, this is after all not a mob book about increasing sales. What I mean is what pain are they already experiencing, not necessarily a physical pain, but a financial one, a psychological one, what is it that is stopping them getting what it is that they need?

Every buyer buys for a reason, some people out of need, some out of desire, some people just because they enjoy spending money, but there is always a reason. It is this need or desire that we explore within pain, your product or service is filling a requirement of some description with your customers, understanding this allows you to gain insights into how your target market spends their money.

Taking the car dealership analogy from earlier, both BMW and Kia soothe a different pain, Kia allows those who desire a new car but haven't got a large budget, whereas BMW fills the desire for those who have money to spend and who want a status symbol. For those who 'need' a car, there are a large amount of used car garages, car auctions or private adverts, the different pains are treated by different solutions, which means all options don't appeal to all people.

We see it every day being advertised, 'no win no fee' solicitors, looking to launch all manner of law suits in your name, what pain is that soothing? Legal help to those who can't afford it, the payoff is higher commission paid to the firm as they are assuming all of the risk, if you could afford good legal advice then the solicitors would be working on an hourly basis and wouldn't really be influenced by the scale of the win.

A good friend of mine was having trouble securing a rental property due to an adverse credit history, unfortunately a CCJ had been levied against him and as a result, despite paying it off four months later, his credit had been badly affected. The problem that that this caused him was whilst attempting to take on a new rental property he was unable to pass a credit scoring process, he had money, a decent job and a partner who earned good money working part time, but still he could not get through a rental credit score. That was his pain, low deposits didn't matter, low monthly payments were not a priority, nice area was desirable but not a necessity, he needed a different process, he required a process that didn't involve credit scoring or had a more varied approach. Having previously owned a property that I rented out I can testify to the fact the a good credit score does not guarantee a good rent payer, yet my friend struggled to find an option. I use this as an example to illustrate that sometimes the most obvious pain you believe everyone suffers is not always the biggest problem effecting whether or not they buy. Explore other issues that could be causing your potential customers issues and focus on that element.

We all have services or products on offer that will appeal to a number of different individuals or businesses, using the other elements included within the avatar model, work out the budget, the age, the geography and that will help you to decipher the pain of your customers.

Chapter 10

Social Media

Finally we have reached stage ten of the avatar and for me it is certainly one of my personal favourites as it's often under-utilised or used wrongly by people who don't understand, either the power of it or how to use it effectively. You may be one of those out there who believes that there is a lots of hype about social media but you have never really seen any results from it, or you may think it's the best thing since sliced bread and your work level has grown massively because of it. The difference between these two points of view is to do with how you use it or understand it.

Firstly what social media is available to the market, Facebook, Twitter, LinkedIn, Instagram, Google +, Foursquare, YouTube etc. there are many more but only a handful are worth spending your time on, that's not to say that use of them all won't expand your customer base, however as with the rest of the Avatar we are focussing in on time spent on a specific task generating the best value for money, remember your time is valuable.

Facebook has become a great tool for business use, most businesses big or small have a Facebook page, in large organisations this is normally being monitored by a very savvy customer service team or marketing company, in small organisations it is usually whoever is responsible for the rest of the admin work, or occasionally the managing director. Facebook however reaches people on a personal level, individuals log on to it every day, in most cases multiple times, so it gives a great opportunity to access customers from different backgrounds including businesses, personalities and individuals.

Twitter is a status writing anomaly; who would have thought that internet stalking would be so popular, this is how businesses and individuals let each other know what is going on and what is important to them. Businesses are continuously posting about what they are up to, sharing pictures and briefs, starting trends through hashtags and getting messages out to the masses. You better believe that large businesses are using marketing companies or customer services to run these accounts for them, every opportunity to capitalise and change the narrative is taken.

LinkedIn is often misunderstood and in some cases treated as a lesser platform, I can assure you that it isn't, it is important for it to be used properly and in the correct way. What I mean is that if you are looking to connect socially with friends or colleagues then it probably isn't right for you, however if you have a business matter to discuss, want advice, want to be noticed as a professional or want to find other professionals, then this is where you want to be. I find LinkedIn to be a very powerful tool within a social media campaign.

Instagram is one social media outlet that I have a limited amount of use of, however I believe that it is more to do with my usage never matching up with the type of program that it is. Instagram relies on the use of pictures; personal photos and celebrity pictures are in common usage on this platform, from a business perspective I believe that you are required to have a particular visual product or if organising an event, pictures from such a source would do very well here.

Google+ is a growing network! it needed to be, there has been so much money spent to make it that way. This platform is all about growing connections far and wide, linking businesses and people all over the world, allowing you to access connections and seeing how they interconnect.

Foursquare is very much a location tool, for businesses who find geography important to their operation, this provides a way of targeting people specifically on their whereabouts. Yet again it is a program that I have rarely used, but that is more to do with the focus of my endeavours never really intersecting with this particular medium.

YouTube, you would have to have been living in a cave for the last fifteen years to not know what YouTube is. It is the ultimate platform for sharing videos, originally filled with media focused on cats doing funny things, this is now a ridiculously powerful tool, regardless of whether you are a singer who wants to get noticed, an up and coming comedian, a large corporation with a new product or Joe Bloggs with a new explainer video, everybody is equal in getting their message to the market. YouTube is set up so you can have your own channel so you can post as little or as often as you like and the best bit is, it is shareable through most of the other social media forums.

So how does this help you with your avatar I hear you ask, well that is very simple, we need to decide upon which one suits your business type and target accordingly. As I said within my descriptions of the main social media platforms I have had little cause to use some of them, mostly because I didn't feel that they fitted the company or product that I was selling, but I can offer up some good example of past uses to help you on your way.

I love LinkedIn and I love it even more when people tell me that they never really got into it, when I am involved in any corporate sales work, I turn straight to LinkedIn, most large organisations have a page or a group on their, once I have highlighted the company I want to target I find their page, on the page is a list of all of the LinkedIn members associated with the company and beside their name is their job title. Having the name and job title of a target customer helps get rid of the first issue of beating the gatekeeper when you pick up the phone, you know who you want to speak too. LinkedIn will also tell you if you are in any way connected to that person through your network of contacts, if you are, you may be able to orchestrate an introduction, if not you can connect yourself to them, I often do this by exploring what LinkedIn groups they are a member of and joining them myself. Once you have that connection you are able to add them and message the person through the site, giving you an opportunity that is ridiculously hard to get if you are just picking up the phone. The groups are another good way to meet potential customers, get speaking to them in a non-pressure format, setting yourself up as the expert and bringing the customer to you. The other advantage is that LinkedIn isn't seen as a social tool so a large amount of organisations have no issue with people having it on at their desk, meaning that these people are more contactable during the day.

When I am launching a new book like this one, I will attack the three big platforms, Facebook, Twitter and LinkedIn, however my target customers are different with the three approaches, Facebook I use to let family and friends know about the book and allow them to share it through their network in the hope I can gain some interest, unless anyone is actually following me it is unlikely that I will gain any sales from just releasing on my page. On LinkedIn I am focussing on the element of this being a business book and I am looking to my connections to take an interest, I will also promote it through any of the groups I'm a member of. My best response will likely be from Twitter however as I am relying on a wildfire approach with the use of hashtags, allowing me get the message in-front of a wide variety of people who may have some interest in my book.

When I was launching a new online delivery service which was based around consumer to consumer I targeted my approach through Facebook predominately, by getting people to sign up to my page and then I was able to constantly keep them updated about what we were doing. This approach worked brilliantly gaining large numbers of interested parties for me to update to.

All three of these platforms offer the ability to promote your products with adverts, normally on a pay per click basis, however the starting criteria I believe is currently higher on Twitter than than the other two.

Using this information you can look at what social media platform is your avatar using, what time of day do they check it, when is the best time to get them on there, what is the best time to post new information or updates? As soon as you are able to ascertain what medium is being used you can focus you time on making sure that when you post content or send messages it will be at a time that the customer will be able to see it and do something with it. Such as LinkedIn is potentially better during the day because people can check it at work, however timing is an important thing, Monday morning is probably not advisable as that's the busy point, Friday afternoon usually means that people have mentally checked out from work so it's not advisable. Facebook & Twitter is more lunchtimes, evenings and weekends, so targeting content at those points is usually a sounder bet.

Social media can change your business if used correctly however it won't happen over-night, so ensure that you are consistent with your approach to social media, little, often and targeted is usually my advice.

Chapter 11

Bring it all together

So now that we understand all the parts of the avatar, I am going to use the example how I approach customer targeting for my consultancy to illustrate how to put the avatar together and give an example of what one should look like.

Location; I have the ability to operate nationally, so if looking for large companies I will expand my search for a national area, however in this instance I am targeting SME's so I am looking for my home town of Milton Keynes up to a radius of 25 miles which can take an hour to travel to. So within my search I will include areas of North Bucks, Northamptonshire, Bedford and Oxford.

Age; as I have said before SME's are usually run by 30-55 year olds, although not exclusively, I would aim to target that specific age group.

Gender; although in the past businesses have traditionally been run more by men than woman, I wouldn't necessarily make that distinction now, so I have no particular gender preference, male or female.

Finance; I have two elements to consider, who can afford a private consultant and who needs to have one. I am offering a free initial consultation and have a range of payment terms that can assist those who have trouble paying straight away, also as I have decided targeting

SME's is to be my approach so I would say finance will not be a major factor, I will be less inclined to target companies with a turnover of less than £100k as they are likely already struggling for a wage and are less likely to recruit a consultant.

Decision Maker; approaching SME's will give me the opportunity to deal with the upper echelons of the management structure, so ideally my customer will be the Managing Director or General Manager.

Knowledge; this is always a difficult concept for a Consultant, as someone who believes that they have great knowledge is likely to look for or accept help from a third party, whereas someone who who has little knowledge may not realise that there is an option to have someone like me come in. So I need to look for someone who is open minded, competent within their business but knows that there are things they don't know. They need to have an interest in business and success they should be willing and able to work towards achieving their goal.

Technology; this may seem obvious but I am looking for forward thinking people, so although of course I expect them to have access to a computer, I will be looking at people who check emails and social media throughout the day, so that means a person with a tablet or smart phone. Although as part of my work I may look for customers to read either other peoples books or my own, I generally look for people with kindle or e-readers, although this is to a lesser extent, it is still worth including to the list.

Interests; so much of my work revolves around helping people get the message out, so it helps if they are already interested in social media and connecting with people in an online environment. It may be cliché' to say you want people who love their job, but for my job it is important that they are fully committed to achieving success so I want them to love their work, it is also how I am more likely to find them.

Pain; for me this is an easy decision, the need or desire for help or improvement, this is where I become most useful, potential customers need to know that they have a problem or be unsure of how to progress an idea and they want to do something about it. This is the real pain required for my avatar to use my service.

Social Media; I will predominately focus on LinkedIn as I know that is where professionals go for connections and possibly help. Although I will use Twitter to help push out blogs or other information, I know my customers will be on LinkedIn.

So there is my person, my customer, in short my avatar is a man or woman, running a business worth over £100k per annum within the Milton Keynes area up to 25 miles, aged roughly around 30-55, that has an interest in business and growth, who regularly checks social media, usually LinkedIn throughout the day or keeps up to date with emails through their tablet or smart phone and is open to reading digital books. They are in need of assistance with an element of growth or survival within their business.

So after the ten steps we end up with a short blurb about the customer, however it is quite specific, I know a good amount of information about what they look like and how my search should be narrowed down. When I set out my marketing strategy, whether it be digital or physical I will refer back to the brief to ensure that it fits in with what my person needs or is interested in, ensuring that all the money or time spent on marketing takes me closer to that person.

This blurb about your avatar can be as big or as small as you like, as long as it is accurate, but also reasonably specific. It doesn't need to be, 'this is Steve, he is an accountant, living on Stafford Grove, he is 32 years old.........' Detail is good but don't narrow it down so much that you can't benefit from other potential sales from someone who isn't Steve. Also if you come out with, 'A person living in a country, on Earth, who has a house ....' Then you're probably not being specific enough, go back and try again.

Remember you can do this activity as often as you like, for every different project you are running your avatar may change, so run through the checklist of ten traits and meet your new customer.

Good luck putting together your avatar it's always nice to meet your customer, even before they know who you are.

If you enjoyed this book you may want to check out;

8 Simple Steps to Business Development

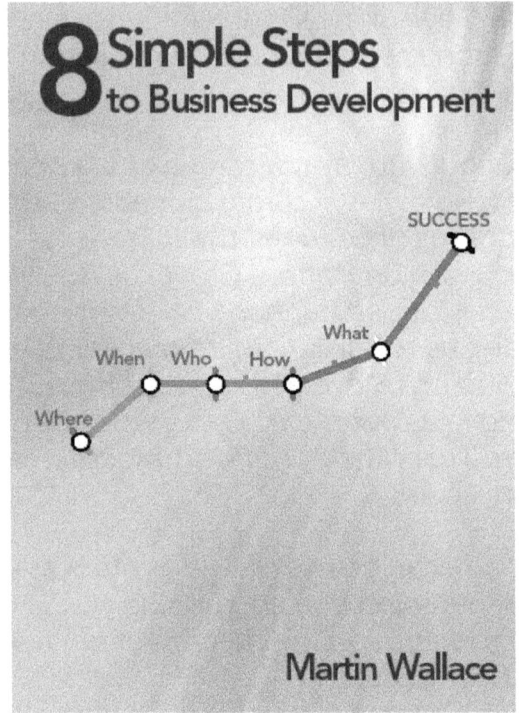

http://www.amazon.co.uk/8-Simple-Steps-Business-Development-ebook/dp/B00ATBDPPW/ref=sr_1_1?ie=UTF8&qid=1426092627&sr=8-1&keywords=8+simple+steps+to+business+development

www.ingramcontent.com/pod-product-compliance
Lightning Source LLC
Chambersburg PA
CBHW071012180526
45168CB00003B/1396